THOMAS CRANE PUBLIC LIBRARY

QUINCY MASS

CITY APPROPRIATION

How Your Body Works

Sending Messages

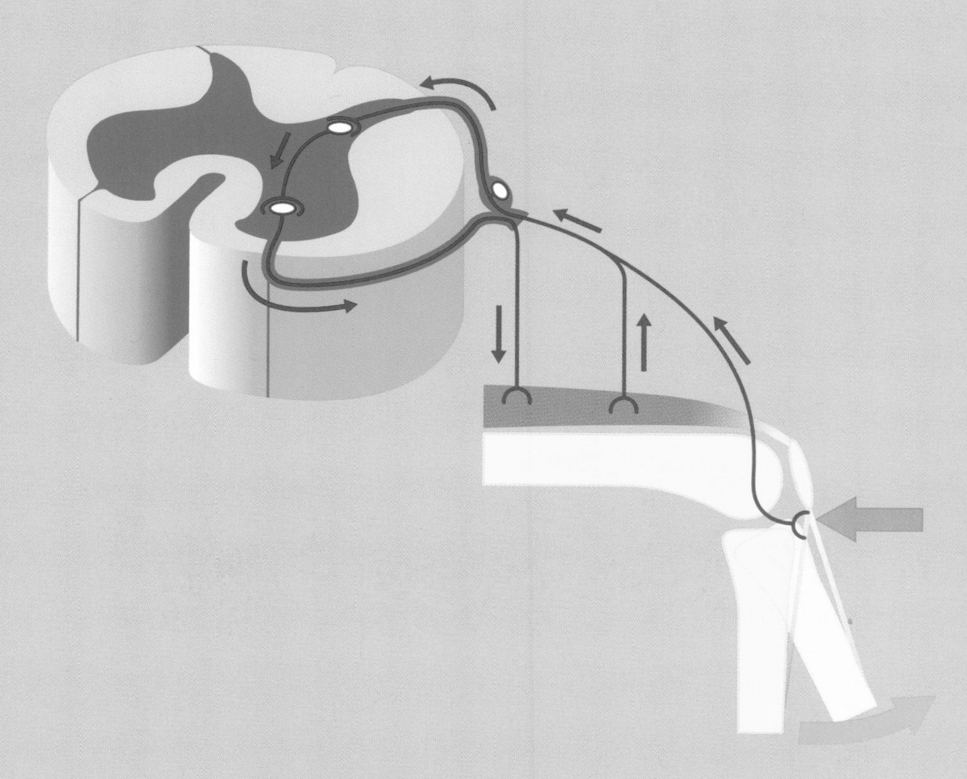

by Philip Morgan

Published by Amicus
P.O. Box 1329, Mankato, Minnesota 56002

Printed in the United States of America, at Corporate Graphics
in North Mankato, Minnesota

Library of Congress Cataloging-in-Publication Data
Morgan, Philip, 1948 Oct. 16-
Sending messages / by Philip Morgan.
p. cm. -- (How your body works)
Summary: "Describes how the nervous system works to send messages in the human body. Includes information about the brain, spine, nerves, glands, hormones, etc. in the body and how they work together. Also explains the development of the nervous system"--Provided by publisher.
Includes index.
ISBN 978-1-60753-055-8 (lib. bdg.)
1. Nervous system--Juvenile literature. I. Title.
QP361.5.M67 2011
612.8--dc22

2010000659

Created by Appleseed Editions Ltd.
Designed by Helen James
Edited by Mary-Jane Wilkins and Pip Morgan
Artwork by Graham Rosewarne
Picture research by Su Alexander
Consultant: Steve Parker

Photograph acknowledgements
page 5 Martial Trezzini/epa/Corbis; 7 Thomas Deerinck, NCMIR/Science Photo Library; 9 Don Fawcett/Science Photo Library; 11 Mehau Kulyk/Science Photo Library; 12 Christine Hanscomb/Science Photo Library; 13 A J Photo/Hop Americain/Science Photo Library; 15 Jonathan A Meyers/Science Photo Library; 17 Wellcome Dept. of Cognitive Neurology/Science Photo Library; 19t BSIP VEM/Science Photo Library, b A J Photo/Science Photo Library; 20 Mark Clarke/Science Photo Library; 21t John Greim/Science Photo Library, b Neil Bromhall/Science Photo Library; 23 Paul Buck/epa/Corbis; 24 Jim Varney/Science Photo Library; 25 Shannon Fagan/Getty Images; 27t JLP/Jose L Pelaez/Corbis, b Tomas Rodriguez/Corbis; 28 Robbie Jack/Corbis; 29 Damien Lovegrove/Science Photo Library
Front cover Mehau Kulyk/Science Photo Library

DAD0037
32010

9 8 7 6 5 4 3 2 1

Contents

Messages and Commands

Your body is a living thing that contains many, many parts, from large organs to tiny individual cells. To make sure that it runs smoothly, important information is sent as coded messages or signals from one part of your body to another.

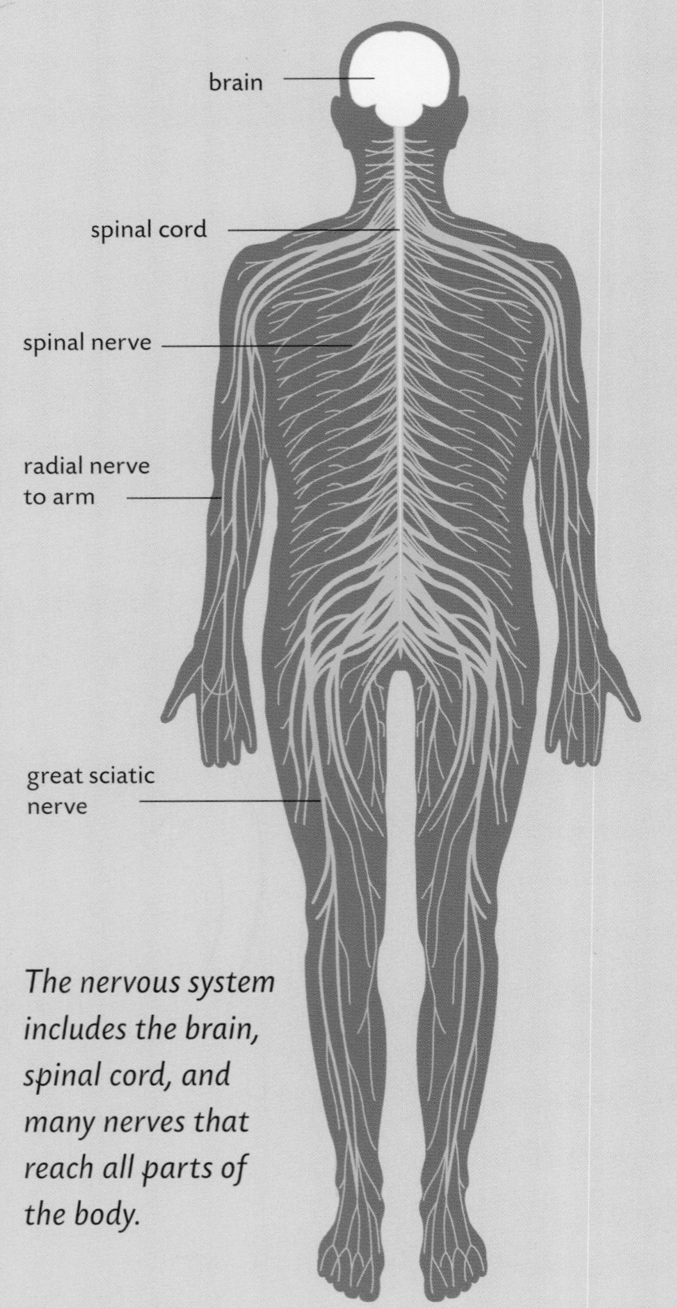

The nervous system includes the brain, spinal cord, and many nerves that reach all parts of the body.

Two Kinds of Messages

Your body sends two main kinds of messages: **electrical impulses** and chemical **hormones**. Electrical impulses move very quickly along nerves. Hormones are much slower because they travel around your body in your blood. In this book, we look at nerves and the nervous system. Then we'll look at the main hormones, where they come from, and how their messages affect the cells of the body.

Buzzing with Electricity

The nervous system in your body is buzzing with electricity. This is not like the powerful electricity in your home, nor the intense electrical crackle of lightning. But zillions of impulses in many varied patterns send all sorts of different messages in every direction. Imagine all the communications systems using every technology—from Morse code and phones to the World Wide Web and satellites—working at the same time to send and deliver information and instructions. The brain sends out

Your brain and nervous system contain many millions of nerves like the cables in this computer center.

commands: Speed up heart! Slow down breathing! Make that muscle contract! Move that foot! Raise that arm! At the same time, your body sends messages back: Left foot hurts! Eyes see plane! Food tastes great! Water is cold! Body is falling over!

Brimming with Hormones

Your blood is brimming with hormones that are released from **glands** that help to control the chemical processes of life, such as growth, development, and **reproduction**. The **pituitary gland** (see pages 24–25) is like the conductor of an orchestra. It organizes these powerful chemicals so that they can deliver their messages correctly.

Did You Know?

The biggest nerve in the human body is the great sciatic (sigh-at-ick) nerve. You have one on each side of your body, starting in the side of your upper hip and running down through your thigh to your knee. Your sciatic nerve is about the same width as your thumb.

All About Nerves

Your body has many kinds of nerve cells. They vary depending on the job they do. But they all have the same basic parts, even though some are long, others are short, and others have lots of branches.

A nerve cell sends an electrical impulse along its nerve axon. The impulse jumps across a tiny gap called a synapse and passes the message it carries on to the dendrite of another nerve cell.

What Is a Nerve Cell?

A nerve cell is called a **neuron**. All neurons have a cell body and a fiber that looks like a string coming out of it. This fiber is called an **axon**, and it carries nervous impulses away from the cell body. A neuron also has one or more "arms" that stick out like branches on a tree. These branches are called **dendrites**, and they receive electrical impulses containing messages from other nerves.

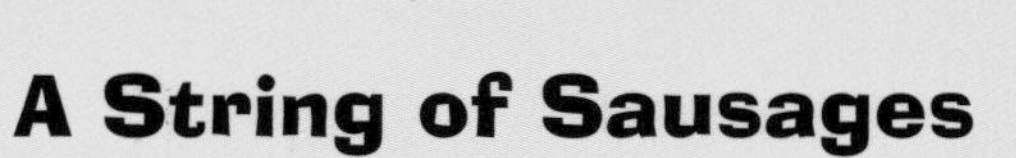

A String of Sausages

Some nerve fibers, or axons, have a white, fatty covering that narrows in places. This makes the fiber look a bit like a string of sausages.

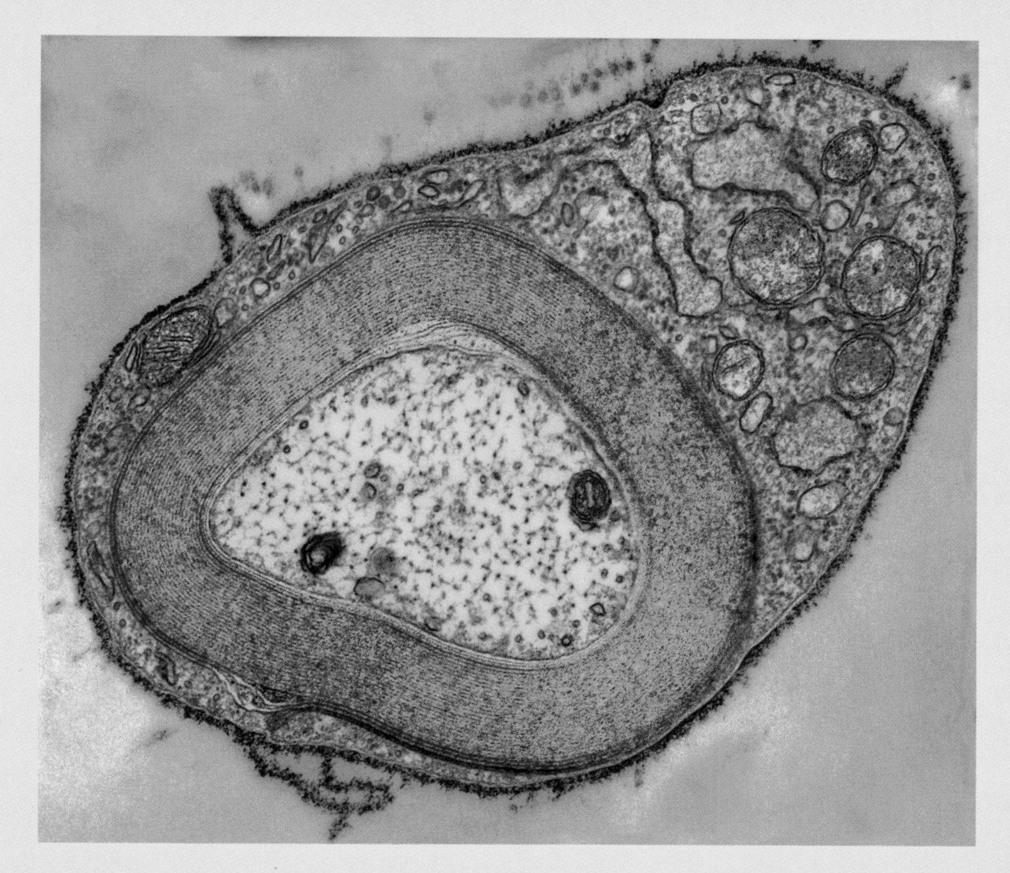

A nerve fiber called an axon (green) is surrounded by a fatty layer (red). This stops the electrical energy of a nerve impulse from being lost.

As a nerve impulse moves along the fiber, it skips from the end of one "sausage" to the end of the next. In this way, it leap-frogs all along the nerve. The fatty covering, which is called a sheath, stops the electrical energy of the impulse from fading away.

Jumping a Tiny Gap

Almost all neurons make connections with each other, especially when they are sending messages to and from the brain and spinal cord.

Neurons don't actually touch each other. Instead, the electrical impulse jumps across a tiny gap called a **synapse** (sin-aps). When the impulse reaches the end of one nerve, a chemical is produced. This moves across the gap in less than a split second to the nerve on the other side.

An Electrical Impulse

Every electrical impulse is the same. It is a tiny electrical current that sweeps very quickly along a nerve. A nerve impulse can travel as fast as 394 feet (120 m) per second along the widest nerve fibers. A nerve fiber can carry messages in only one direction, but some can carry as many as 200 impulses every second.

A Vast Network

Every part of your body is linked into a vast network of nerves. The most important part of the network is your brain and spinal cord. Together, these form your central nervous system. Nerves from your brain control your face and head, while nerves connected to the spinal cord control the rest of your body.

Bundles of Fibers

Most nerves are bundles of nerve fibers, wrapped up in fatty tissue (see page 7). There are two types of fiber: **sensory fibers** and **motor fibers**. Sensory fibers send messages to the spinal cord and the brain from a part of your body. Messages could be from your skin, a sense organ such as your nose, or an internal organ such as your lungs. Motor fibers send messages from your brain and spinal cord to your muscles, such as the calf muscle in your leg. As you grow older, you learn to control the messages these fibers send.

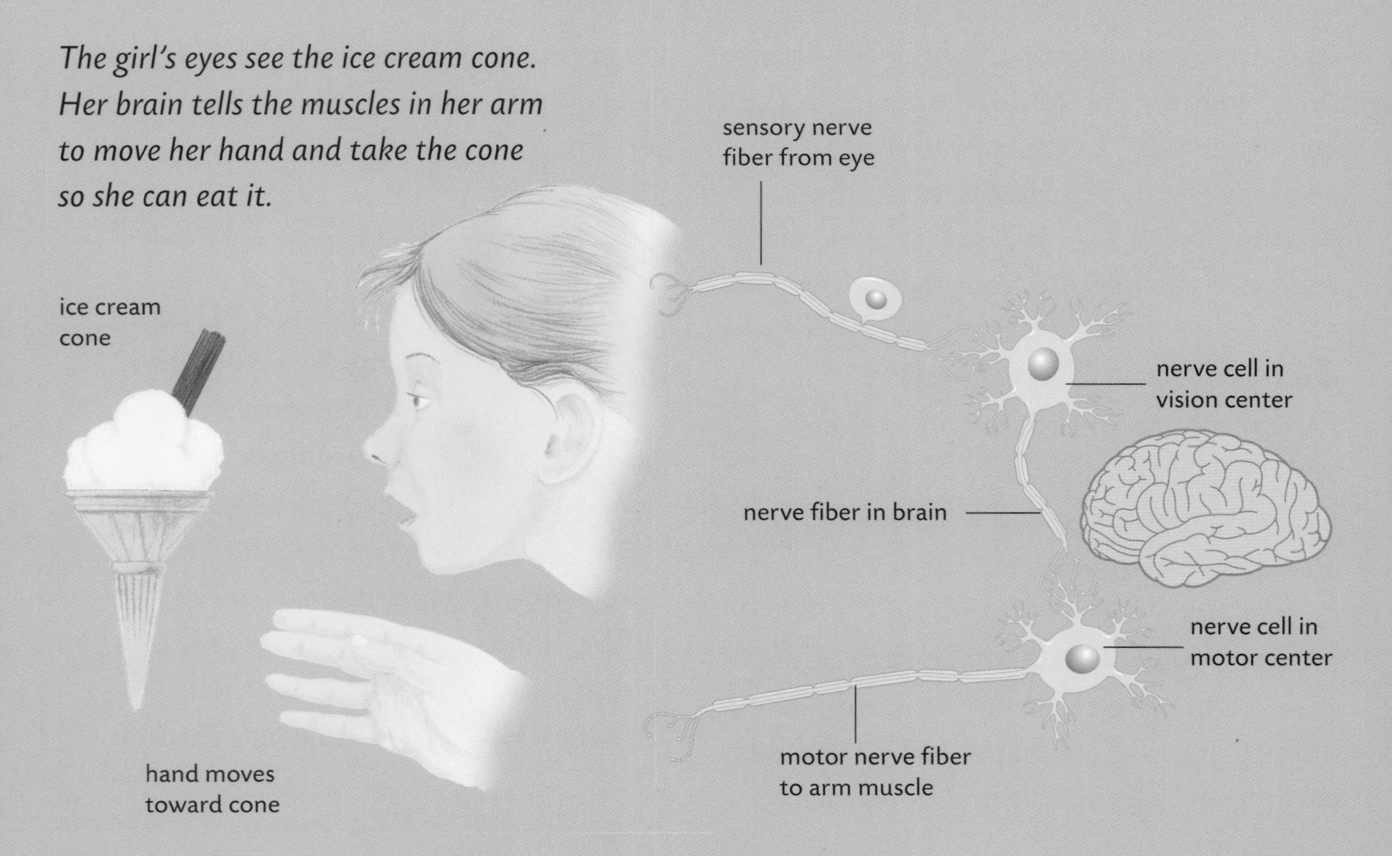

The girl's eyes see the ice cream cone. Her brain tells the muscles in her arm to move her hand and take the cone so she can eat it.

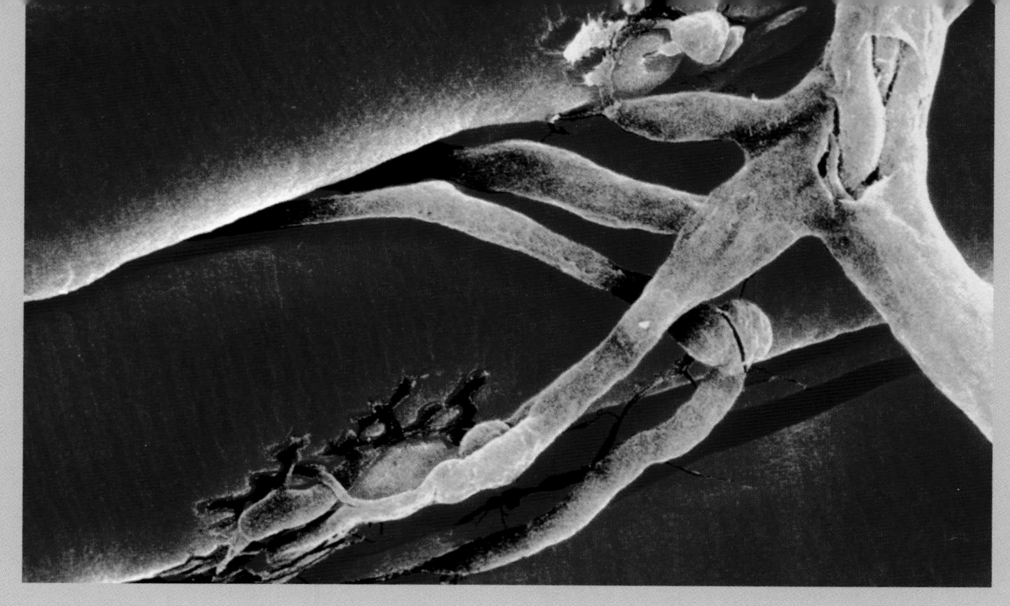

The ends of a motor nerve fiber (green) connect to muscle fibers (red). Impulses from the nerve tell the muscle fibers to contract or relax.

Automatic Nerves

Some nerves act automatically, which means you can't control them. They form a system that has two parts: **sympathetic nerves** and **parasympathetic nerves**.

Your sympathetic nerves work hard when you're active or in a stressful situation. They widen the airways in your lungs, speed up your heart, open the pupils in your eyes, and make your saliva thick (see pages 28–29). They can even make your hair stand on end!

The parasympathetic nerves work more when you're relaxing or even sleeping. They often have the opposite effect to the sympathetic nerves. They slow down your heart, narrow the airways in your lungs, and speed up the movement of food in the intestine. They can also make the tear glands in your eyes produce tears.

HEALTH CHECK
Nerve Tests

An injury or an illness, such as diabetes, can damage a nerve. Doctors may test a nerve by measuring how well it passes on an electrical impulse. The doctor holds a probe against the nerve and stimulates it with a safe, painless electrical current that is picked up by an **electrode** further down the nerve. A computer measures the speed of the impulse to determine whether there is any damage.

Your Spinal Cord

A super communications highway carrying a massive number of messages runs down your back, from your head to just above your hips. This is your spinal cord. It contains millions of nerves that are connected to your abdomen, arms, and legs through 31 pairs of spinal nerves.

Protecting the Cord

Your spinal cord is a long white bundle of nerves that is connected to your brain. An adult's spinal cord is as thick as a pencil and grows up to about 18 inches (45 cm) in length, which is about as long as the lower arm, from the elbow to the fingertips. The spinal cord is protected in several ways. Most of the protection is from your spine, a strong chain of bones called **vertebrae** (ver-teb-ray) that is longer than the cord. Inside the bones, the cord is wrapped in three layers.

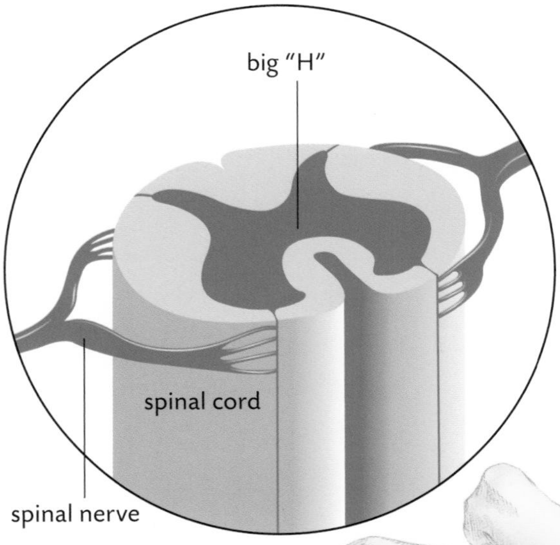

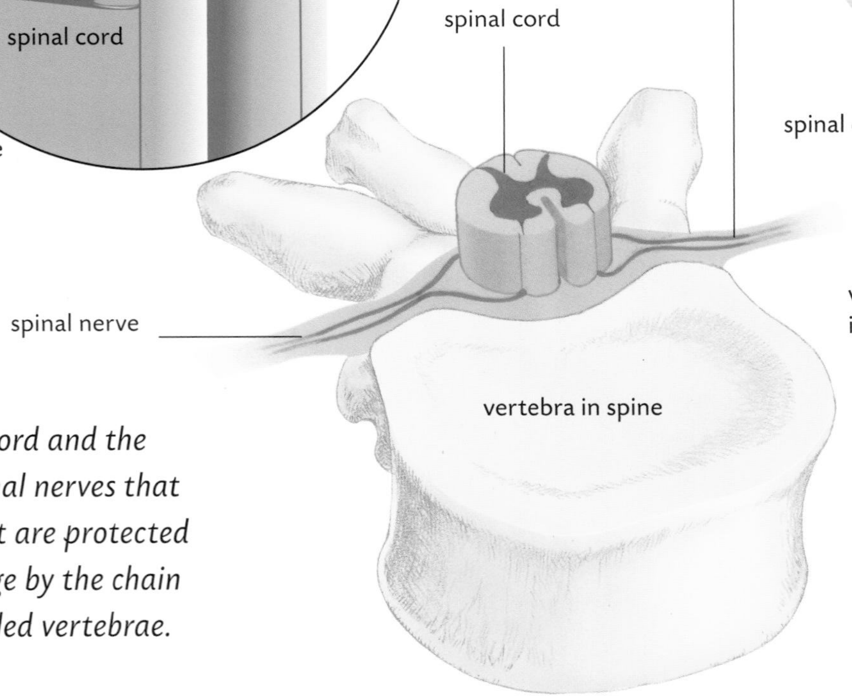

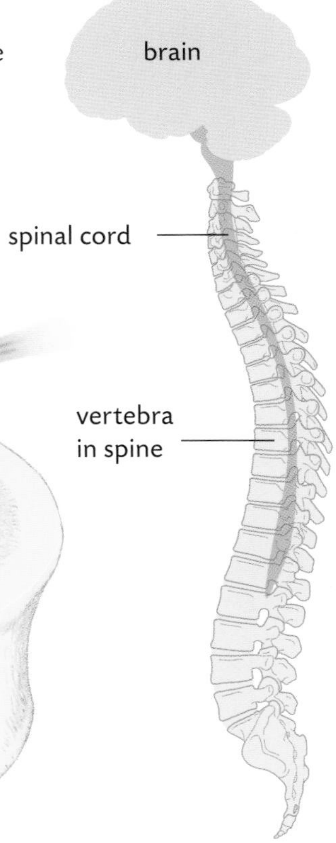

The spinal cord and the pairs of spinal nerves that come from it are protected from damage by the chain of bones called vertebrae.

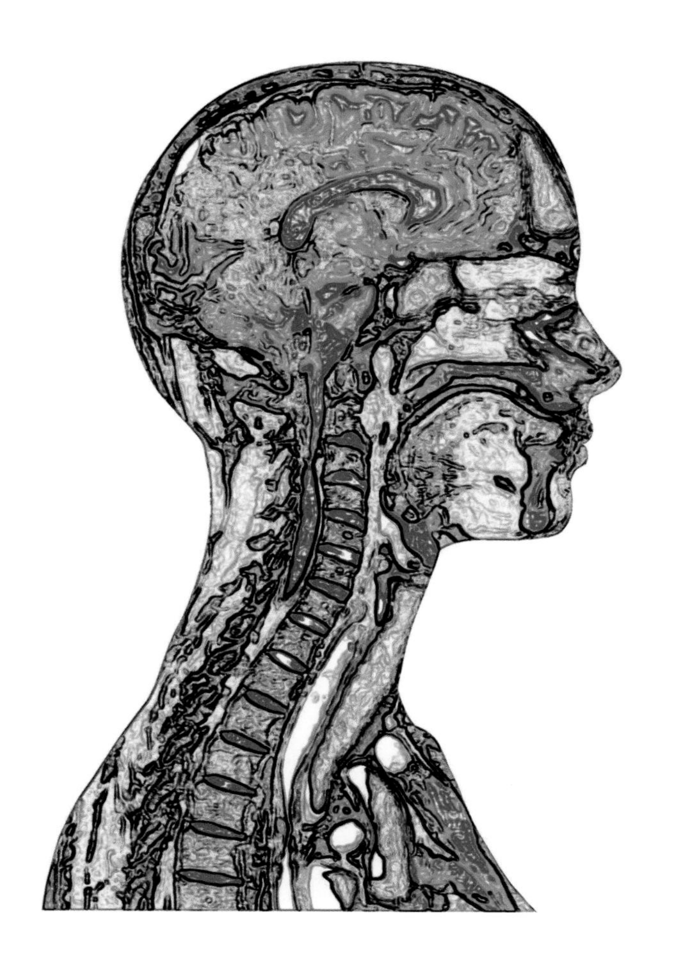

In this body scan, you can see the brain, spinal cord, and vertebrae of the spine.

Between two of the layers is a liquid called the **cerebrospinal fluid**. Together, they cushion the cord against all kinds of shocks and bumps.

The Big "H"

If you could cut a spine in two and look at the tissue, you would see a big gray "H" surrounded by white mass. It also looks a bit like a gray butterfly.

The "H" contains all the cell bodies of the neurons in the spine, and the white mass contains all the axons (see page 6). In the middle of the horizontal bar of the "H" is a canal filled with cerebrospinal fluid, which brings food such as glucose to the nerve cell bodies.

Groups of Neurons

The gray part of the "H" contains three groups of neurons. One group receives detailed messages from the body about sensations, such as temperature and touch. For example, imagine you are blindfolded and you dip your finger into warm water. Touch and temperature messages travel to the brain via these sensory neurons. Your brain instantly identifies these two sensations as "warm" and "water."

The second group of neurons carries motor nerve messages from your brain to the skeletal muscles of your body, telling them to contract so you can move. The third group contains neurons that help control your organs, such as your kidneys.

Did You Know?

Your spinal cord doesn't grow as long as your spine does. This means that an adult's spinal cord is only two-thirds of the length of the spinal column of vertebrae.

Reflex Actions

When you touch a hot radiator, you quickly draw your hand away. If some food becomes stuck in your throat, you cough it up so you don't choke. These actions are called reflexes, and they happen automatically, without you having to think.

You have other reflexes, too. When the food you chew moves to the back of your mouth, you swallow it. You sneeze if something is stuck in your nose.

Amazing Babies

A baby is born with lots of reflexes: it sucks a finger that touches the roof of its mouth or its lips, and it cries when it feels hungry or thirsty. During their first few months of life, babies have a diving reflex when they go underwater. A flap called the epiglottis automatically closes to stop water from entering the lungs. When a baby's head goes back, it spreads its arms and legs and opens its fingers—this is called the startle reflex. If you stroke a baby's palm with your finger, it will grasp it firmly. When a baby is about six weeks old, it loses several reflexes and starts to control its movements.

At only a few months old, a baby has a diving reflex to help it swim underwater.

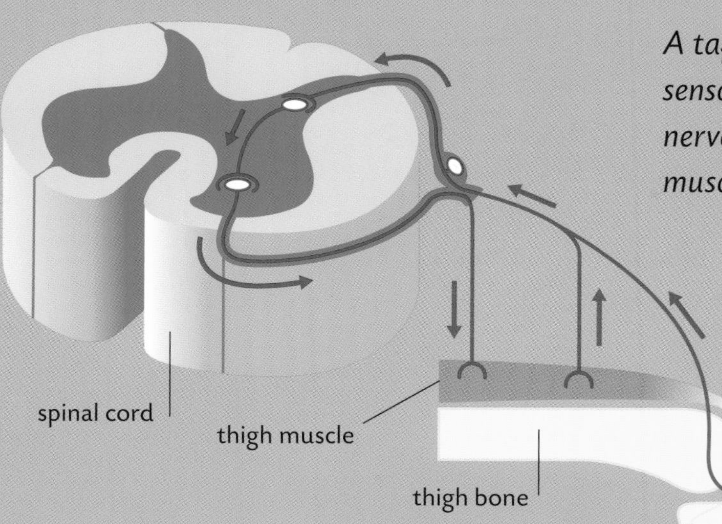

A tap on the ligament below the kneecap sends sensory messages to the spinal cord. A motor nerve sends a message back, telling the thigh muscle to contract. This raises the lower leg.

No Brain Required!

The messages in a reflex travel from the spinal cord, not the brain. A reflex needs to use the shortest route so the response is as quick as possible. If you touch a hot radiator with your hand, pain messages go from temperature sensors in your skin to the nearest neurons in your spinal cord. This sends a command message to the muscles of your arm and hand, saying: Move your hand away now!

Knee Jerk Reflex

A **ligament** links your kneecap to your shinbone. If you rest one leg on top of the other and firmly tap the ligament, your leg and foot jerk forward. This is the knee jerk reflex, and the messages go first to the spine and back (see above). A doctor may perform this simple test to make sure your spinal reflexes are working normally.

A doctor tests a boy's knee jerk reflex by tapping the ligament below the kneecap.

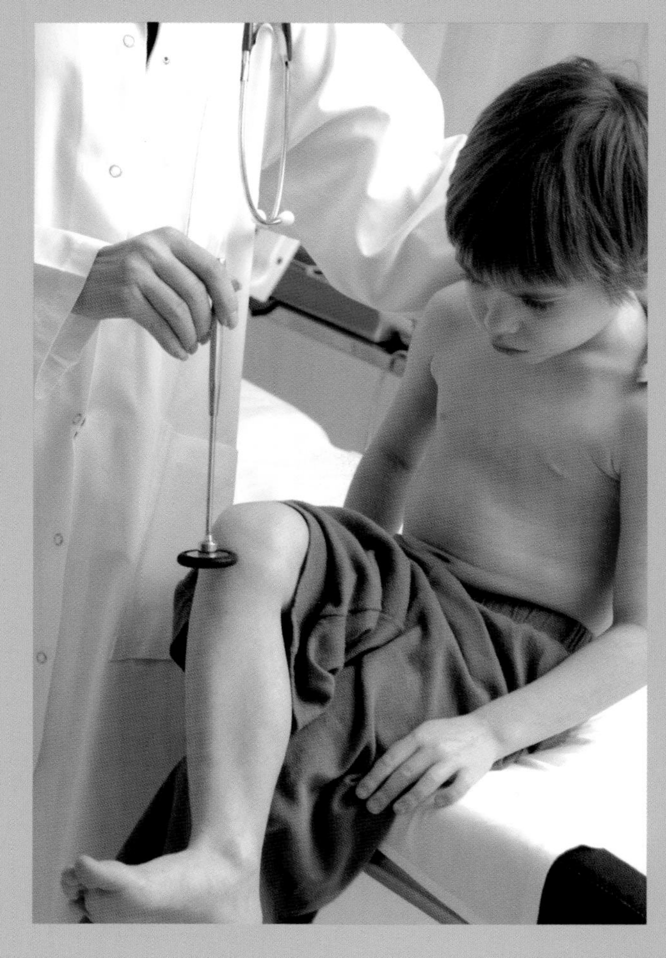

Your Brain Is Boss

Your brain is the central headquarters of electrical impulses. As well as controlling much of what goes on in your body, it's where you do your thinking, feeling, imagining, and remembering.

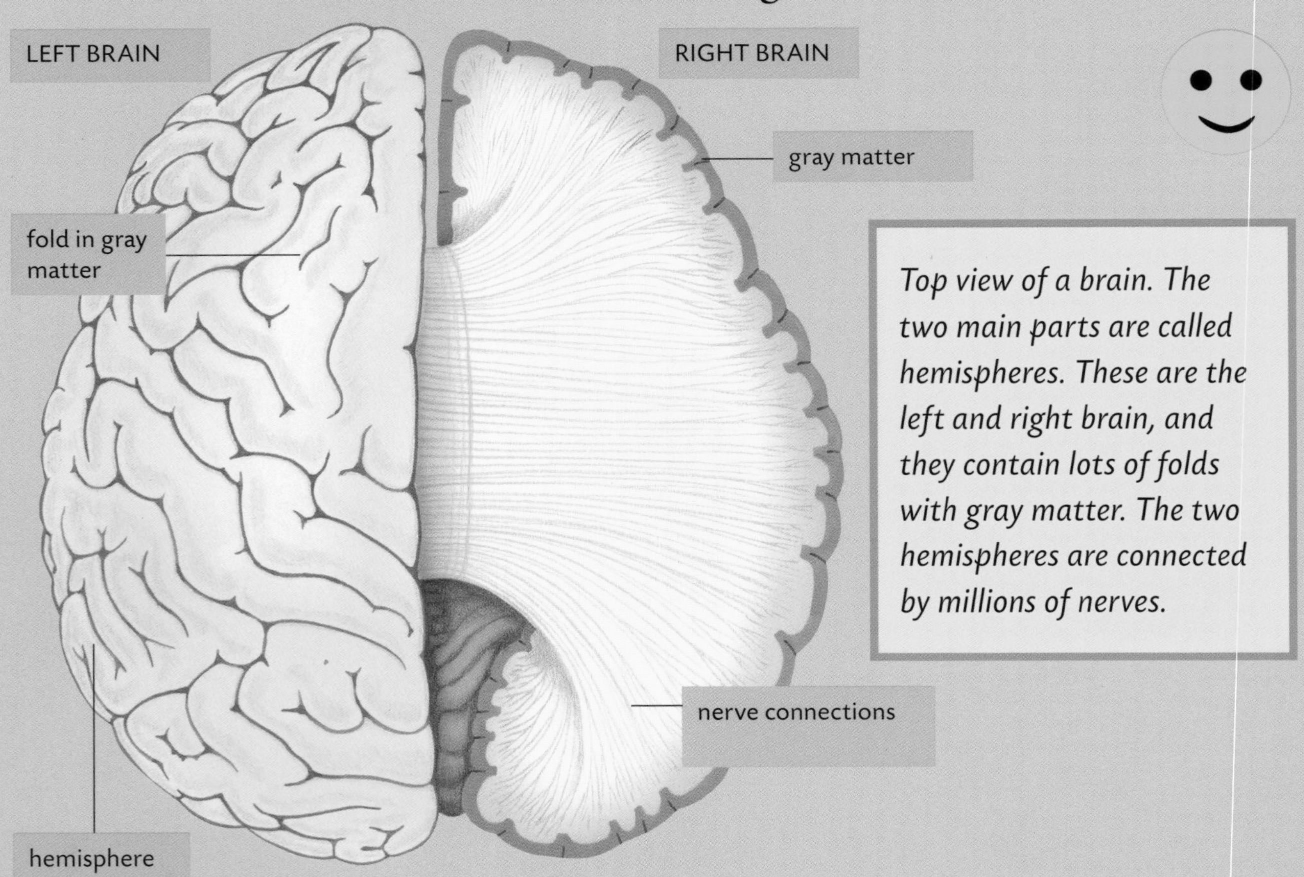

Top view of a brain. The two main parts are called hemispheres. These are the left and right brain, and they contain lots of folds with gray matter. The two hemispheres are connected by millions of nerves.

Clever Computer

No one has ever counted the number of nerve cells in a brain, but medical scientists think there must be at least 12 billion, with another 50 billion supporting cells called glial (glee-al) cells. They make lots and lots of connections with each other, which is why we think of the brain as a clever computer.

The size and power of our brains makes us intelligent. The many connections between the nerves in your brain are very well-organized—they help you to remember a friend's face, speak in different languages, see millions of different colors, complete a crossword puzzle, play the violin, and feel happy, sad, or bored.

Right and Left Brains

The biggest part of your brain is the **cerebrum**, which has a thin layer of gray matter that covers the left and the right parts called **hemispheres**. This gray matter is where your brain does most of its thinking, makes sense of all the messages that come from your body, and sends out a mass of commanding messages in response.

Did You Know?

An adult brain is soft and squishy and weighs about 3 pounds (1.4 kg). A brain needs a huge amount of glucose and oxygen to work properly, so up to a fifth of the blood in your body goes to your brain. This is more than any other part of the body.

The right side of the brain acts on sensory messages from the left side of your body and controls the movement of your left side. The left brain acts on the sensory messages from the right side of your body and controls the movement of your right side.

The two hemispheres are connected by lots of nerve fibers in a structure called the corpus callosum. The connections mean that the left side of the brain knows what the right side is doing, and vice versa.

Painting a picture is one of many complicated actions that we do with the help of our brains.

A Map of Your Brain

Medical scientists have mapped most of the regions of the brain, so we know how many of its amazing nerve cells are laid out and what each region does.

Four Lobes

The cerebrum (see page 15) that covers each hemisphere has four areas, or lobes (see right). The frontal lobe behind your forehead holds groups of neurons that help you think and feel emotions. The temporal lobe on the side of your brain is where you hear noises. It helps you tell the difference between sounds and also helps with your memories.

The parietal (pa-ry-et-al) lobe on the top of your brain helps you interpret sensations such as pain (see pages 20–21), temperature, and touch. At the back of each hemisphere is the occipital (ok-sip-i-tal) lobe. This is the vision center where your eyes send messages about what they see.

Underneath the occipital lobe, at the back of the brain, is the cerebellum. This is a large area of the brain that helps you make precise movements. It helps you make skilled movements, such as playing a guitar, and to perfect your balance, when you dance or play sports, for example.

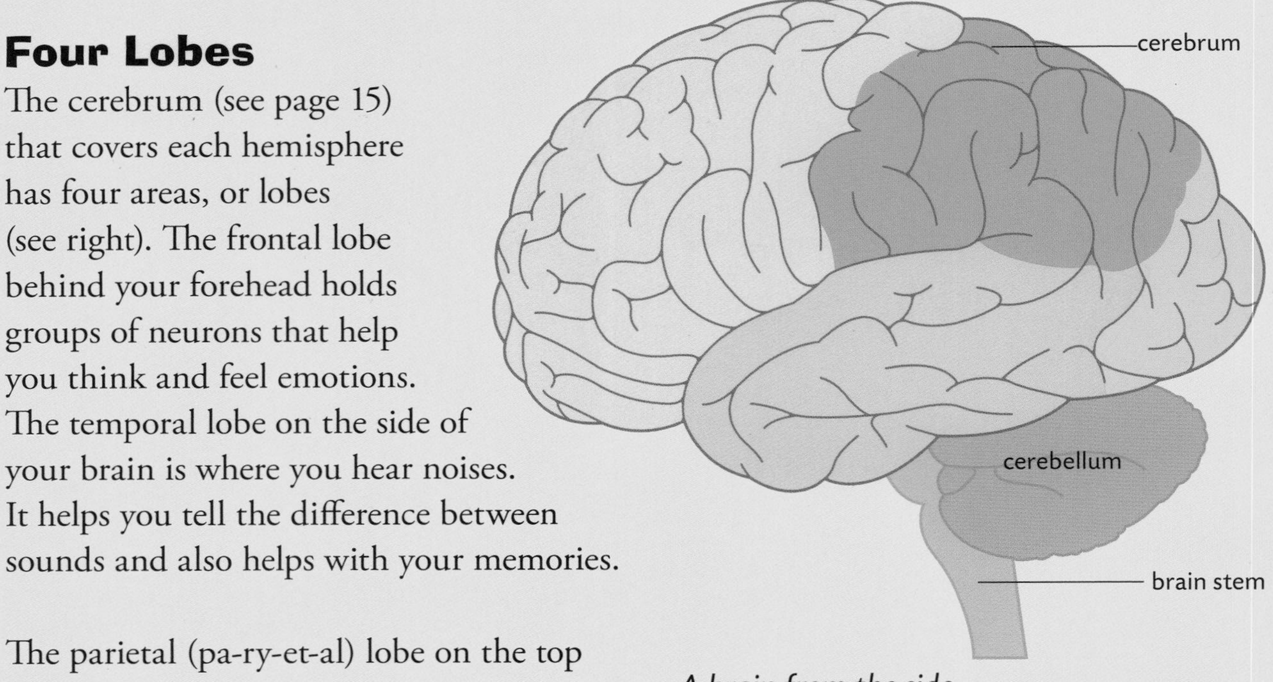

A brain from the side.

- *frontal lobe*
- *parietal lobe*
- *occipital lobe*
- *temporal lobe*

Vital Control Centers

At the base of your brain and between the two hemispheres are several control centers. These are for sorting out all the nerve impulses carrying important information. The brain stem is where the spinal cord meets the brain, and this is where nerve cells control your heart rate, breathing rate, swallowing, and blood pressure. Above the brain stem is a vital center called the **thalamus**, which is a relay station for all kinds of messages. It receives and sends out sensory messages between the key regions of the brain.

WHEN THINGS GO WRONG

Unusual Brain Activity

When doctors think someone's brain is starting to go wrong, they may use a PET scan to look for unusual activity in the brain's cells. The PET scan can help them decide where the problem is, and also to find the cause of the disease. PET scans can detect tumors that are a sign of cancer. They can also spot patterns of activity that might mean someone is suffering from depression.

Watching the Brain

Today, scanners help doctors see how our bodies work. One, called a PET scanner, allows doctors to watch the brain and see which areas are active when we talk, hear, and think. A patient has an injection of a harmless radioactive substance, which goes into their brain. The PET scan then shows these areas on a screen (see below).

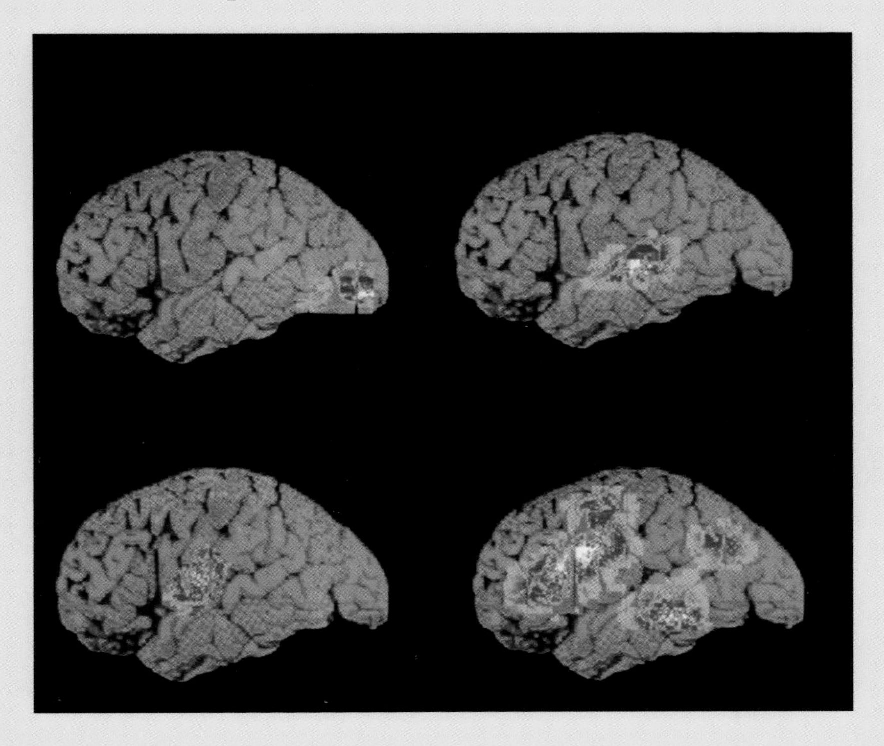

PET scans show areas of the left brain that are active during four tasks, colored yellow, orange, and red. Top left: areas active when we see. Top right: areas active when we hear. Bottom left: areas active when we speak. Bottom right: areas active when we think about and speak verbs.

Brain Waves

Your brain is active 24 hours a day, seven days a week. Millions and millions of electrical impulses whiz between the various areas of your brain, even when you're asleep, so your brain is always buzzing with brain waves.

Recording Brain Waves

Brain waves show the electrical activity of your brain. There are four main types of brain waves, called alpha, beta, theta, and delta waves (see below). Your brain produces alpha waves when you are awake but not doing much, beta waves when you're concentrating, theta waves in deep meditation or drowsiness, and delta waves when you're in a deep sleep.

We can see these brain waves when doctors attach electrodes to the skin on a person's head and face and connect them to a machine called an electroencephalograph (ee-leck-tro-en-seff-alo-graff) or EEG. The machine can detect the brain waves because they create electrical impulses that come through the skull to the skin. The machine records the waves as spiky patterns on a computer screen.

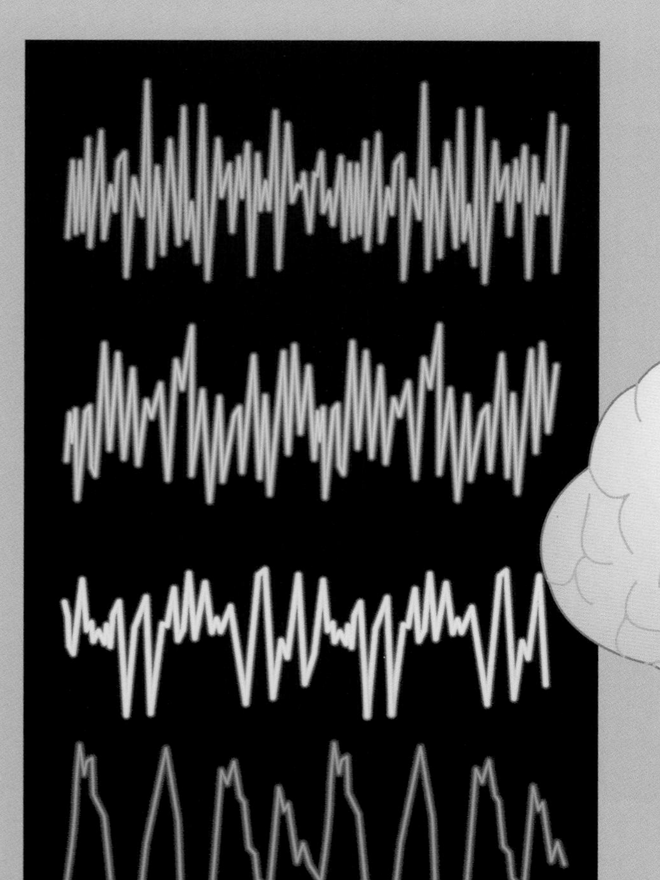

The four types of brain waves are fast alpha and beta waves (top two) and slower theta and delta waves.

Did You Know?

When you are asleep, your brain goes through the same cycle about every 90 minutes. First, you sleep deeply, and your brain's activity slows down. Then you sleep more lightly for a while—your brain becomes a bit more active, your eyes move, and you start to dream.

During Sleep

An EEG shows that the brain waves of a person who is falling asleep are close together and shallow (see right, number 3). During deep sleep (see right, number 5), the waves are more spread out and taller. During another part of sleep called REM sleep (see right, number 6), the waves are not as regular and become very shallow.

REM stands for rapid eye movement, because your eyes move rapidly from side to side, even though your eyelids are closed. Some muscles in your body may start to twitch and your breathing becomes quicker and more shallow. During REM sleep, you may have lots of dreams.

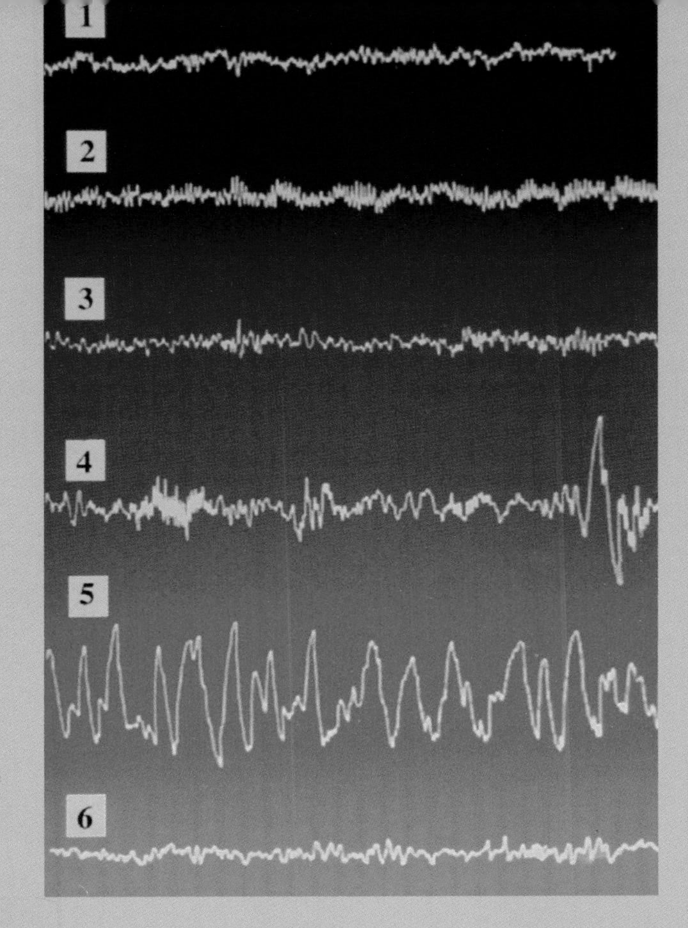

EEGs of brain waves while awake (1–2) and during sleep (3–6).

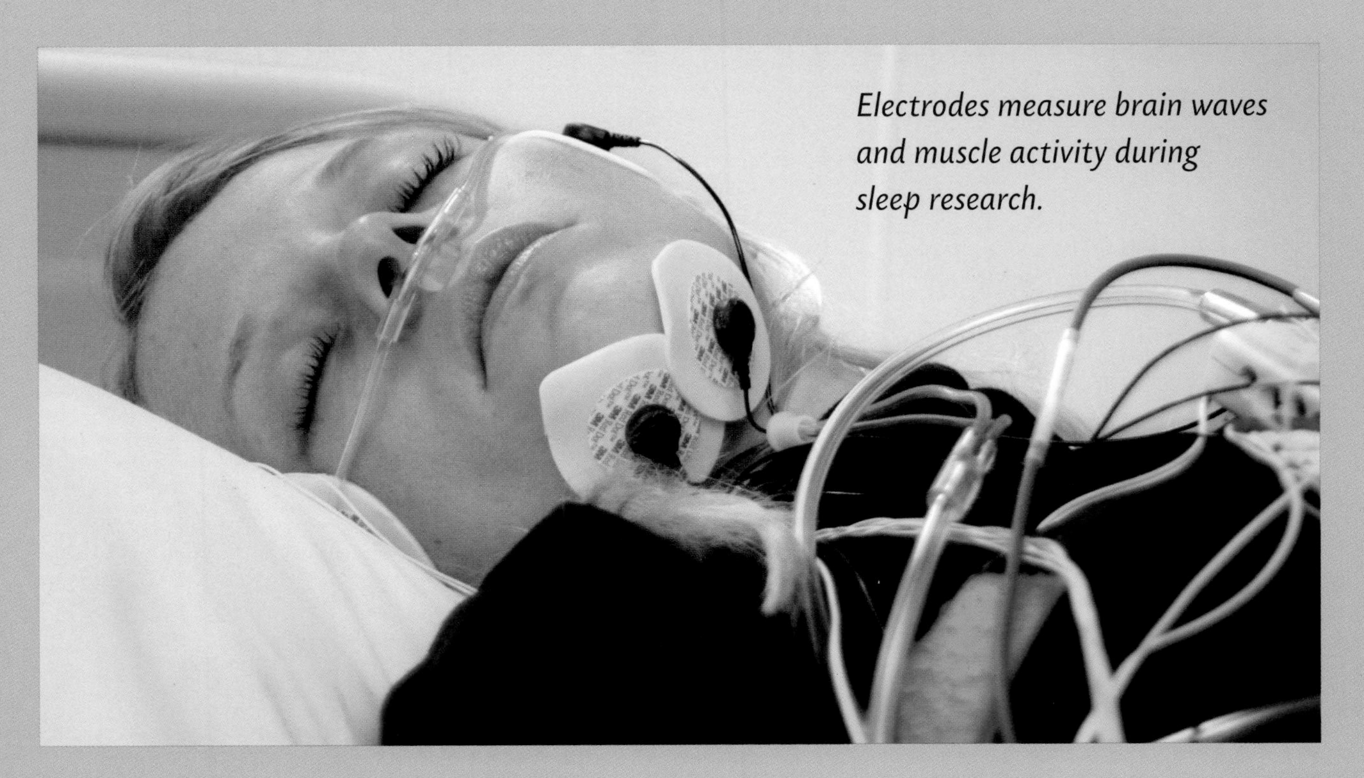

Electrodes measure brain waves and muscle activity during sleep research.

Ouch! That Hurts!

Everyone knows what pain feels like. When someone pinches your skin, you feel a sharp pain. A problem with a tooth can cause a dull throbbing ache in your jaw. Injuries and disease also cause pain when they damage cells, tissues, and organs.

Feeling Pain

Pain messages are carried as electrical impulses by special nerve fibers from cells called pain receptors. We have these all through our bodies. Sensitive areas of the body, such as the skin and tongue, have lots of pain receptors, but the internal organs, such as the liver, have only a few.

Most of the nerves that carry pain signals don't have a fatty sheath around them. So the pain signals travel more slowly than other signals—several feet per second, compared with 394 feet (120 m) per second for the largest nerve fibers.

Nerve impulses take about one sixtieth of a second to travel from the feet to the brain, but pain signals take between half and one second to reach the brain.

Numbing the Pain

Several drugs can stop you from feeling pain by blocking the pain signals as they pass along nerve fibers. These chemicals are called **anesthetics** (an-ess-thet-icks), and they stop you from feeling any sensation, including pain.

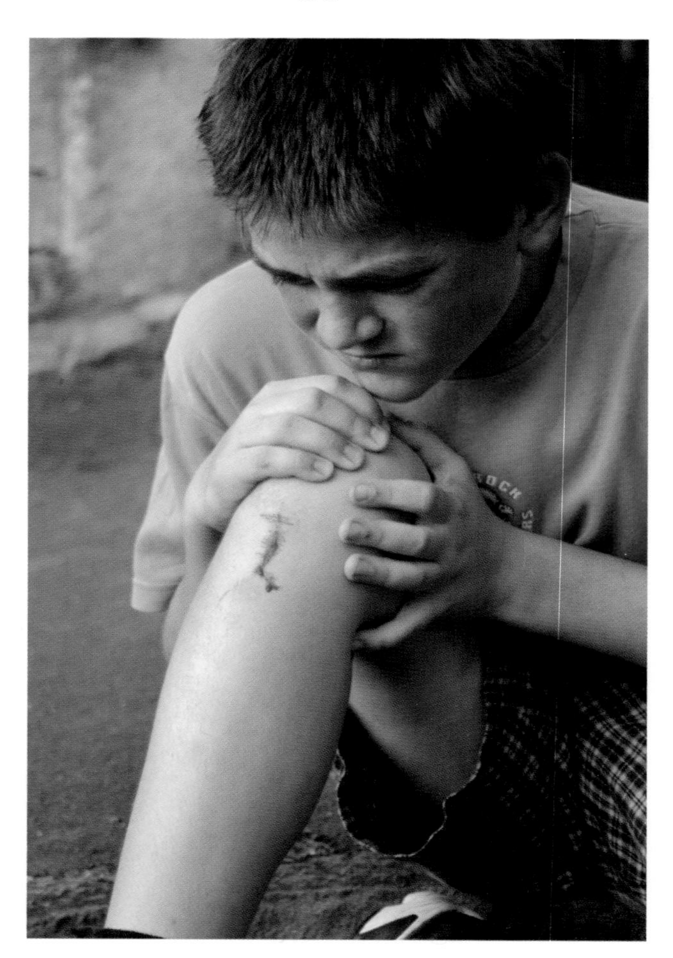

When you fall over, you may not realize you have cut your knee right away, and then you see that it is bleeding.

Your whole body goes numb if you have a general anesthetic, and you lose consciousness for a time. People having major operations, such as heart surgery, need a general anesthetic. Local anesthetics numb a small part of the body. Dentists inject a local anesthetic into your jaw to numb the nerves that lead away from a tooth they need to fill.

When a woman has a baby, doctors often use anesthetics to numb the pain she feels. One form of local anesthetic can be injected into the spinal cord so that it numbs the nerves in the pelvis and legs. This is called epidural anesthesia.

Anesthetics can be breathed in as a gas, as a general anesthetic during an operation, or as a shot given to relieve pain when giving birth.

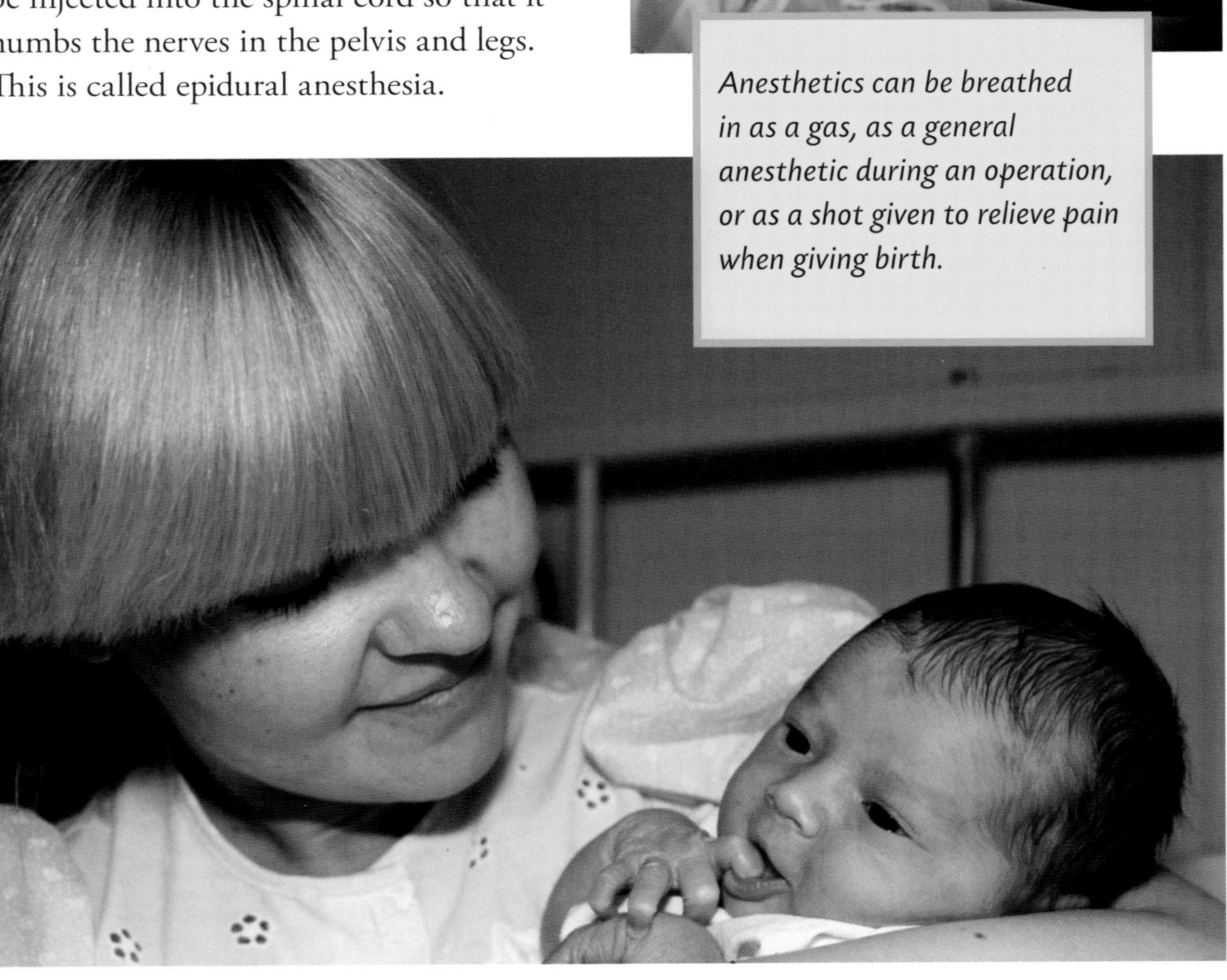

Chemical Messengers

Your body makes powerful chemical messengers called hormones that control the way it works. These hormones are made in glands and are released into your blood to carry instructions to particular parts of the body.

Two Types of Glands

Your body contains many tissues, called glands, which make and then release a special liquid. The word gland comes from a Greek word meaning acorn. Some glands, such as salivary or sweat glands, release their liquids into a channel called a duct. Other glands release them into the blood so they travel all around the body. These are called the endocrine glands and their fluid contains a hormone that has an effect on particular cells in the body.

Glands and Their Hormones

Your body has several endocrine glands. The most important is the pituitary gland (see pages 24–25). This is below the **hypothalamus** under the front of

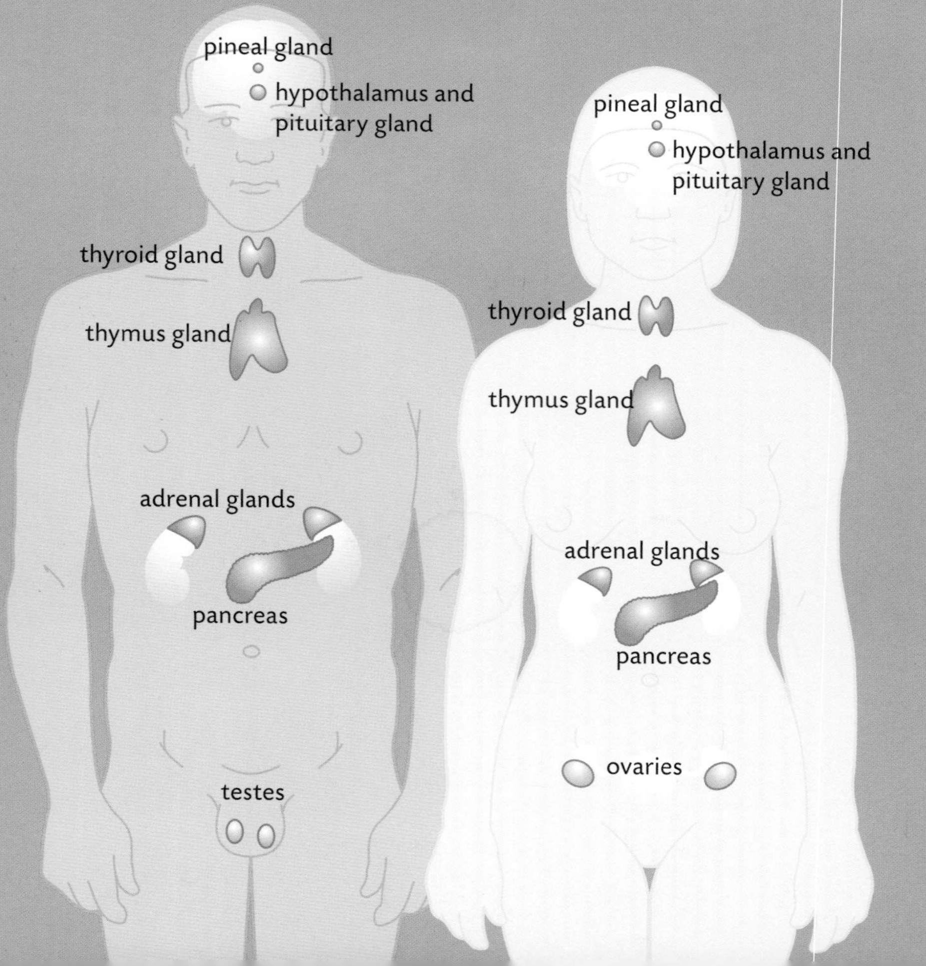

The position of important endocrine glands in a man's body (left) and a woman's.

the brain. It makes its own hormones and helps control other endocrine glands, too.

Your thyroid gland sits in front of your windpipe at the bottom of your neck. It makes a hormone called **thyroxine**, which helps the cells of your body get energy from food. Your pancreas is a gland behind your stomach. It makes two hormones (insulin and glucagon) that make sure you have the right amount of glucose in your blood.

You have two adrenal glands, one on top of each kidney. These make **adrenaline**, which prepares your body for danger and stress (see pages 28–29). The adrenal glands make other hormones that help your body use carbohydrates, proteins, fats, and salt from your food. They also make a hormone called cortisol, which your body releases when you are hurt.

In men, the two testes make testosterone, which helps produce sperm. Women have two ovaries that make estrogen (e-stro-jen) and other hormones. Your body begins to release these hormones—testosterone in boys and estrogen in girls—when you reach **puberty**.

WHEN THINGS GO WRONG

Not Enough Thyroid Hormones

If someone's thyroid gland does not produce enough hormones, especially thyroxine, everything in the body slows down. The person may have very little energy and can put on a lot of weight. This problem usually affects people over 40, although some babies are born with it. People who have the problem take thyroid hormones.

The hormone testosterone allows men to grow a beard and makes their voices deeper.

The Master Gland

The pituitary gland is your body's master gland. It controls all the other endocrine glands by sending messages that tell them to start or stop making hormones. It also works closely with the hypothalamus above it in the brain.

Communications Center

The hypothalamus and the pituitary gland form one of the most important communication centers in your body. The hypothalamus is part of your brain and is about the size of a lump of sugar. The pituitary gland, which hangs down from it on a short stalk, is the size of a small pea. They work together, so the brain controls the hormones your body produces and then the hormones have an effect on the brain. This communications center is the main place in your body where nervous impulses and endocrine hormones meet. This means that some hormones can affect your mood, feelings, and thoughts, while feelings such as fear and rage can change the way your body makes hormones.

Everyone experiences different moods, and sometimes they are caused by changes in the hormones, for example, at puberty or in adolescence.

Keeping Watch

The hypothalamus controls your body's temperature, appetite, and thirst. Meanwhile, the pituitary gland makes its own hormones and controls how others are produced, such as adrenaline. Together, they keep watch on what is happening in your blood. Does it have the right amount of glucose? Does it have enough water or too much? Is it warm enough, or is the temperature falling or rising? Is there enough adrenaline and all the other endocrine hormones?

The pituitary and hypothalamus make and send chemical messages all the time, not just to other endocrine glands, but also to many other parts of the body.

Some parents keep track of how fast their child is growing by regularly measuring their height and marking it on the wall.

Growing Up

The pituitary gland makes hormones that control your body's growth. During childhood and **adolescence**, it makes a growth hormone that helps cells divide, for example, making your bones grow longer and your body taller.

Some of the pituitary gland's other hormones are messengers that tell your organs of reproduction to produce their own hormones. In women, these organs are the ovaries, which produce the hormone estrogen. In men, the organs are the testes, which produce testosterone.

Very Tall People

Very occasionally, someone's pituitary gland makes too much growth hormone, so the bones of the body continue to grow. This is what has happened to very tall people. It is called pituitary gigantism. In September 2009, a 26-year-old Turkish man called Sultan Kosen, who is 8′1″ (2.47 m) tall, became the tallest person in the world.

How Hormones Work

Endocrine glands release hormones into the blood when they're told to—often by messages sent from the pituitary gland. When each hormone reaches particular cells in the body, the hormone tells them what to do.

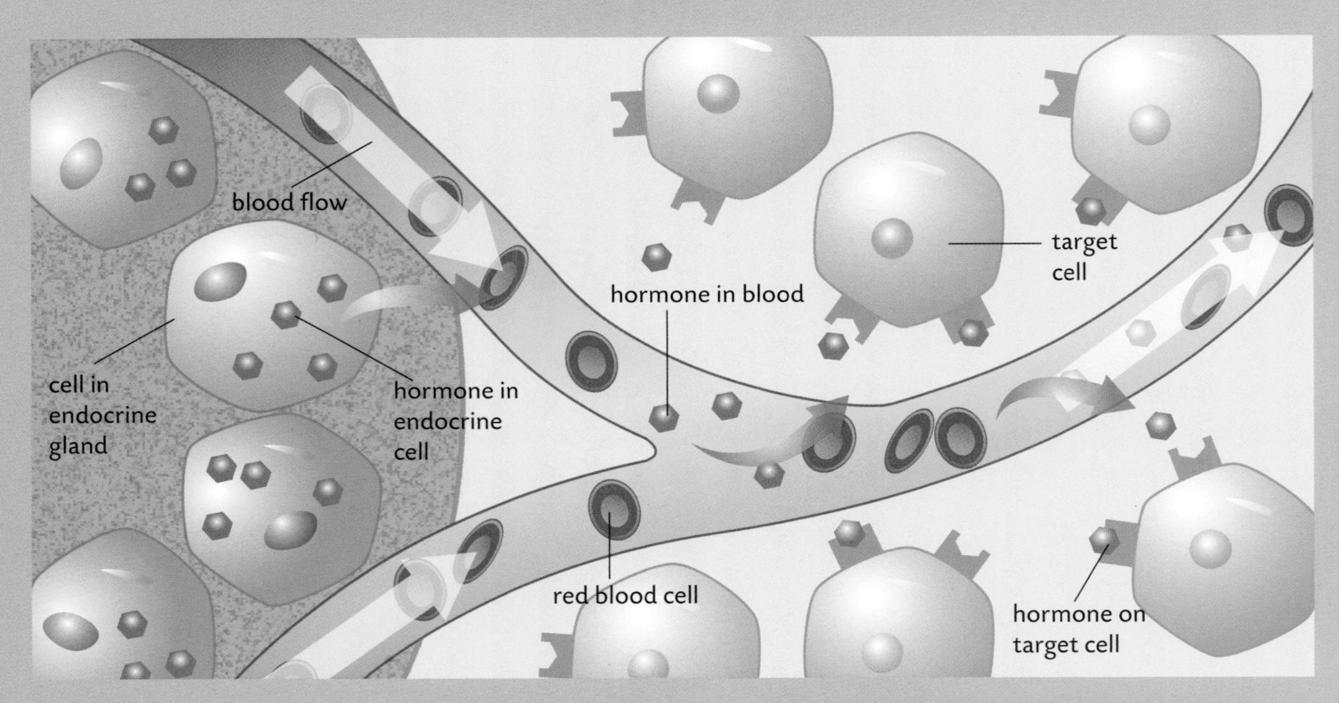

Hormones leave an endocrine cell and travel in the blood. When they reach their target cells, the hormones lock onto the target cells.

Full of Hormones

Your body can keep track of all its chemical messengers. Your blood is always full of hormones of one sort or another. At any one time, there might be short bursts of adrenaline, a steady stream of growth hormone, and messages being constantly pumped out and sent back to your pituitary gland.

Target Cells

Every hormone is a chemical messenger. It goes to a group of cells, called target cells, and delivers a message: Do this! Do that! Make this! Make that! Stop this! Stop that! For example, insulin goes from your pancreas to your liver and tells its cells to store glucose. At another time, glucagon leaves your pancreas and goes to the same liver cells to tell them to release glucose into your blood.

Hormones only deliver their message to their target cells. They do this in a way similar to a key turning in a lock. Hormones have their own unique 3D structure. This is the key that fits into the lock, which is in the **membrane** around the target cell.

Feedback Loop

Your body has a system for starting and stopping the release of hormones from their glands. It's called the feedback loop.

When the pituitary gland spots that your body needs a particular hormone, it sends a chemical messenger to the right gland to tell it to start releasing the hormone.

For example, the pituitary gland notices when your body needs a hormone called thyroxine. This is made by the thyroid gland in your neck and helps the cells of the body get energy from food. Your pituitary gland sends a thyroid-stimulating hormone (or TSH) to the thyroid gland, telling it to make more thyroxine and release it into the blood. When the amount of thyroxine in the blood reaches the right level, the hormone tells the pituitary gland to stop sending TSH.

If your thyroid gland doesn't make enough thyroxine, you may feel tired. This hormone usually helps your body's cells make energy, which keeps you alert.

Fight or Flight

Adrenaline gets your body ready to deal with danger and stressful situations. This is known as the fight or flight response and it shows how nervous and chemical messages work closely together.

Performing on stage in front of an audience can be very stressful.

Ready for Action

When you are in danger, your body goes into action immediately and prepares to deal with the danger: either you fight it or run away. Your brain senses the danger and sends urgent nerve signals to your adrenal glands to produce adrenaline. The signals come through the sympathetic system of nerves (see pages 8–9).

The same thing happens when you are in a stressful situation, such as performing in public for the first time. Most people become anxious and feel butterflies in their stomach as their body makes and releases lots of adrenaline.

HEALTH CHECK
Symptoms of Stress

When people feel overwhelmed by problems or lead lives that give them no time for rest, a doctor may check for physical symptoms of stress. These might be tiredness, headaches, high blood pressure, muscle pain, mouth ulcers, and catching more infections than usual. The doctor may recommend a stress test on an exercise machine to measure someone's heart rate, breathing rate, and blood pressure.

What Happens to Your Body

Adrenaline speeds up breathing and makes your heart beat faster and more powerfully. This sends more oxygen-rich blood around your body. It also releases huge amounts of glucose fuel for your muscles to use, and releases stress hormones from another part of the adrenal glands.

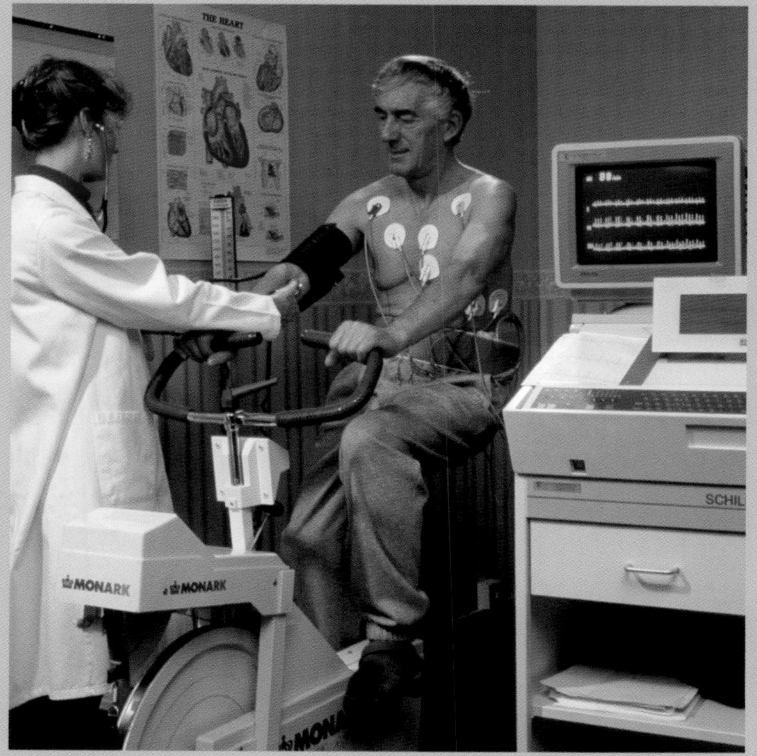

A stress test can reveal how your body responds to intense exercise.

At the same time, the messages traveling through the sympathetic nerves send more blood to your brain and muscles to help you think clearly and move swiftly. Less blood goes to your stomach and intestines, so your digestive system slows down. The pupils of your eyes widen so more light can enter and you see better. Your lens focuses on objects further away rather than things close to you. Your saliva becomes thick and sticky.

Glossary

adolescence The time when children grow and develop before becoming an adult.

adrenaline A hormone from the adrenal glands that helps speed up breathing and the heart rate.

anesthetic A chemical substance that stops you from feeling pain.

axon The long fiber of a neuron that carries nerve impulses away from the nerve cell body.

cerebrospinal fluid A clear, watery fluid that nourishes your brain and spinal cord and helps to protect them from injury.

cerebrum The largest part of the brain. It has two hemispheres, many folds, and nerve connections with all parts of your body.

dendrite A branching part of a neuron.

electrical impulse A tiny electrical current that moves very quickly along a nerve fiber.

electrode A small, metallic device that picks up an electrical current and carries it to a piece of electrical equipment.

gland An organ that makes fluids or chemicals, such as hormones.

hemisphere One of the two halves of the cerebrum in the brain.

hormone One of the chemicals that act as messengers in the body. Hormones help control the way the body works and develops.

hypothalamus An important tissue above the pituitary gland and below the thalamus at the lower front of the brain.

ligament Strong, elastic tissue that connects one bone to another.

membrane A very thin layer that can be inside or around a cell or can be a protective covering for a row of cells.

motor fiber A nerve fiber that carries electrical impulses through the central nervous system and to the muscles.

neuron A nerve cell.

organ A major part of the body that has one or more special tasks. Your heart, lungs, liver, kidneys, eyes, and ears are all organs.

parasympathetic nerves A network of automatic nerves that help control your body as you rest or sleep.

pituitary gland The master gland of the hormone system.

puberty The time when a child's body changes into the body of an adult.
reflex A muscular action, such as swallowing, that you do automatically without thinking about it.
reproduction The process of making and having babies.
sensory fiber A nerve fiber that carries electrical impulses from the sense organs, such as the eye, to the central nervous system.
sympathetic nerves A network of automatic nerves that help to control your body when it is active or feeling stress.
synapse A tiny gap between nerve fibers.
thalamus An important part of the brain where sensory messages are received and sorted.
thyroxine A hormone made by the thyroid gland that helps the cells of your body get energy from food.
vertebrae The bones that make up the spine.

Books

Ballard, Carol. *The Brain and Nervous System* (Exploring the Human Body). KidHaven Press, 2005.

Burstein, John. *The Astounding Nervous System: How Does My Brain Work?* (Slim Goodbody's Body Buddies). Crabtree Pub., 2009.

Houghton, Gillian. *Nerves: The Nervous System* (Body Works). PowerKids Press, 2007.

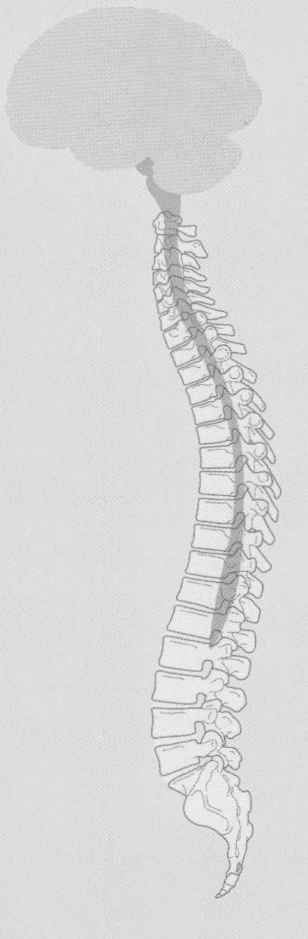

Web Sites

www.pbs.org/wnet/brain/
Read all about the secret life of the brain: its history and anatomy as well as memories, feelings, and illusions.

http://faculty.washington.edu/chudler/introb.html
Discover a whole lot more about your brain and spinal cord and the way your nerves work.

Index